REAL ESTATE REALTOR KNOWS HOW... THE EASIEST PATH TO THE BIGGEST CASH

David Wong
Real Estate Realtor Knows HOW…The Easiest Path to The Biggest
CASH

Published by BooxAi

ISBN: 978-965-577-987-5

REAL ESTATE REALTOR KNOWS HOW... THE EASIEST PATH TO THE BIGGEST CASH

DAVID WONG

CONTENTS

REAL ESTATE realtor knows HOW
The Easiest Path to The Biggest CASH!

Focus on Team Works, Team Spirits, Team Efforts and
Team Earning

Either be a Leader or Follow a Leader

BY

DAVID Y. WONG

INTRODUCTION

This book is written for Real Estate in A systematic way of finding qualified buyers and sellers into a day-to-day routine, working toward from a single realtor to building an empire to fulfill a satisfactory career.

This book is for general reference only. The materials and information here are not provided for the purpose of professional or legal advice. The author assumes no responsibilities for errors or omissions in the content of the book.

In my opinion, every Real Estate office should have a book for their individual agent for learning and growing and expanding their capability to know the Brokerage well and share offering their best knowledge and offer available options to their client to be served hand in hand

In Real Estate, a house or a home is a commodity that it sells by itself based on the conditions, locations, and price.

A great realtor knows how to deliver, execute the solution and find abundance of business because they have A system.

This is a highly rewarded in remuneration and very well professional business to be in and yet is very dedicated hard work efforts. As much as important for the buyer and seller to decide whom they like to work with for their largest investment in Life. (Why?)

Real Estate realtor is based on the act between buyer and seller as a middle person to put a final deal together in the manner of a service.

Successful well runs Brokerages or individual agent or any cooperate business, which must have a great system in place and constantly upgrade, mortify, and update.

A good system entails a good plan, good people, and good tools.

This information' and shared knowledge will take us in-depth inside the real estate world of knowing what needs to be done to get a solid rock bottom foundation, building the core for many years to come.

A system built for people's desires for living with freedom in financial world and happiness and a healthy lifestyle and for helping the client or common people.

A great system brings predictable results, foreseeable results, workable results, rewarding results, fulfilling results, happy results, plus many more good reason results.

Introduction to FAST path to build A system in Real Estate for day-to-day living is based on a real-life experience; this book is about to discover or find YOUR true path to success!

Setting a realistic expectation from the start of the career in Real Estate for each appointment to take place either on listing side or buyer side is ever important; however, this book contains more working towards on listing side, the reason will attract or landed up more with many buyers and sellers.

The last thing you want to do with a new client is NOT to scare them out of their decision to buy or sell by telling them how confusing the market changes constantly.

Q: Why learning skills and knowledge are important?

A: Have a clear target WHO and WHY!

The key is striking a balance to make it clear what they are getting themselves into the whole process and reassuring them from the start by showing them how you'll guide them to gain the benefits and, what you need to offer with full disclosure and, what do they expect from you during and after the entire endeavor.

Let's begin to understand some KEY things here.

Three Main Options / Reasons:

1. Address the concern, fear, or regret beforehand or move forward with a clear proactivity to calm their fear.

2. If they certainly decide to discuss openly the possibility of slowing down or stopping the process, you can remind them that this was going to happen, and it is alright to do so rather than hidden surprises.

3. If it is too much for them to deal with----emotionally, financially, or otherwise you want them to know now, before you invest your precious time in working with them.

You need to put yourself into their shoes to try to understand the questions as they need the answer honestly and the feelings, they need to be comfortable.

Don't forget you work in this industry every day. You have seen the hot market on the seller's listing that gets 20 different offers at one time. You have dealt with the insecurities of buyers who are afraid they are overpaying or are they qualified with the mortgage finance?

You know today's market is so crazy.

The key concept is: If you win...I win a little if you lost ...I lost more. (Realtors know what I'm talking about!)

Rules:

If you know how, what, and when, you are in a much better position to work with rather than dealing with the unknown (Do you agree?).

By the end of the book, you probably know how, what, and when to work on A system!

First, look at all Preparations before the appointment.

SECTION 1

THOROUGHLY READY OR ABLE TO DO SOMETHING

1

———————

PREPARATION, PREPARATION AND PREPARATION:

On the market update, always review the past activities or past 12 months, the current time plus for the future room to expand. (Given the right circumstance)

Focus on a new resolution or new plan or road map as a guiding tool.

Understand the market trends inside and out from the activities daily, weekly, monthly, or yearly.

Set a workable goal and stick with it no matter what, as always find an accountability person or a role-play partner to work with.

Start up with everyday preparation on daily routine focus on prepare what is important, what needs to be done on 1st priority

Everything doesn't always go according to plan, a constant unexpected change development but to prepare well ahead is to create the most productive results. Such flexibility and adaptability are a sign of the strength of a professional.

Inside this blueprint, we will learn each step of the

way that its so crucial every move, left or right will lead us to the higher probability of closing the cap

Defined your own referral program or rewards:

For example: Free trip vacations reward, VIP gifts, net-work celebrations for appreciation year-end party, special bonuses, and surprises incentive program for life-time referrals.

Who are your preferences?

Choose the A, B, C client's preference to work with.

For example: Work with a client who is willingly and easily to accept and workable and coachable with A system. Not everyone is on the same page unless they see the true value in them.

Understand the client's reference and fall into A system, building the data based to identify who are the buyers and who are the sellers or investors specifically and classified as such:

A: AAA excellent client.

B: potential to upgrade client.

C: on the mailing lists / follow up client.

Building a strong new work moving forward. Asking clients for a full testimonial is essential along with a good picture as vice verse offering to help them to grow their business whatever it takes.

For example: A clients were in the blinds and curtain business which is related to the real estate home accessary, both types of business can expand their ideas to grow together. (As always, to offer the exchange value to increase production sales.)

This will save us a lot of time and perform much more effectively, not only benefit to the realtor as well as the clients. (Who doesn't want it)

Some realtors put in the 110% of hard work and time and effort but gain no reward.

Other realtors put in 1% of little work but get a big reward.

How has that happened, we always asked, and we wonder why?

This is a real world and reality, welcome to the beautiful and yet challenging Real Estate career.

Working with A system in place will take us to a far and predictable and enjoyable business operation. (You walk the talk)

Opportunities don't come every day, not every time as always, but we create it, we make them happen, and we take a proactive move and see it in front of us and we need to know how to grab it. (A system)

Reference Box:

Key: We do not need many clients that we cannot handle, rather than a hand full of quality clients that build an ever- lasting relationship and have a great financial relationship that builds wealth together for a lifetime in the same goal mindset. (isn't it what we all want?)

The worst is never prepared enough, it reflects on or shows on our faces, and it looks like widening the cap of closing the sales.

The beauty of the good preparation is way ahead of many of our competitions and it looks easy closing at the end of the sales.

e.g.

Imagine we were late in showing up for the appointment!

(How does that make us or the client feel?)

We are all busy preparing for our vacations, wedding ceremony, friends and family get together, events or anniversary, but most often we rush and rush for an important meeting without preparing enough and expecting the good results (wonder why?).

Our experience showed:

Detailed check with each aspect of the appointment.

Clear our doubts instantly when obstacles arise.

Take notes of everything so that it would come in handy at a later point in time.

It looks good even in a short meeting, without showing any distraction.

Overall, our attention is fully focused and show enthusiasm, no messages, no text, no phone calls. (to show we care for the business meeting)

We are 100% pure for the client's attention

All winners are preparing more than ever...

Next, what study has to do with A system!

2

STUDY

The purpose of reading a good inspired and motivating book will bring us to the next level to open more choices to choose from finding a path that suits us the most for building a systematic way of our career.

A truly lifelong career depends solely on A system.

To study puts us in a better position to know what we need to know in advance, knowing the goal with an action plan will guide us all the way to reach the goal we set.

As realtor knows that their income relies on commission solely, to avoid the roller coaster ride or feeling up or down on our emotional stage sitting and waiting for the next paycheque to arrive or not knowing where the next cheque or deal is coming from or not able to fulfill the transaction, would NOT be a fun time at all in which might be created a negative ripple effect. (Stay away as much as possible)

Study shows way back to the history in the 80' to 90' the was the sales rule called 80/20

80% of the realtors are working hard to get 20% of the business.

20% of the realtors are dominated by the 80% of the business.

As the current time evolved, thing has changed.

It's become more dramatic in the sales rule called 95/5

Imaging the top 5% of the top producer are gaining the 95% of the business, which in return working more efficiently, more effectively and get a much more predictable income and much higher income.

What happens to the 95% realtor? Going after the 5% of business.

Why? Does it have to be like this?

Because of the A system!

The beauty part is everyone can build A system on their own term. (How?)

Here, with A system to follow, the success rate is more perceivable.

Study and practice increase confidence, when confidence is increased eventually increases sales + increase income.

Let's investigate study entails:

As a realtor before an appointment:

We study the dept of the market condition in all aspects, telling us what the value of the marketing price is by doing a comparative market analysis (CMA).

We study the recently sold property (CMA).

We study the current activity on the market property (CMA).

We study the expired listing on the market (CMA).

We study who is the most active listing realtor in the area.

We study who our competitor is.

We study who is the main buyer in the area.

We study how we can win over the sales appointment.

If we know what we know, we are ahead of others

And

We must practice the scripts.

We must practice the role-play (Q and A).

We must practice asking closing question.

And

We build the level of confidence by studying this:

We know and define what's our purpose of the presentation (is to sign a contract).

We know what defines a qualified appointment (by asking the right question).

We know and having the courage to ask for closing, said yes (let's work together or let's move forward) or no (I'm not able to do this job)

We know and define as a professional realtor what exactly the client is looking for at the end of the conversations.

Do we know what is the most important thing that the clients always ask? And want?

For example:

What is the price am I getting?

How long does it take you to sell?

What is the marketing plan you have?

We know what we know will give us a different way to work with.

Studying and gaining skills and knowledge is the only way to offer more in this present time and is our day-to-day agenda.

Consumers buy or sell based on decisions made on emotional feeling attachment. (If they like it, they will buy or sell)

In today's world, telecommunication, information

technology and green energy approach are many people are concerned, if we can utilize the availabilities or obtain the uses, we'll be able to help to increase the confident for providing the sales decision is all part of the service to offer.

A system will make it right most of the time at any time anywhere with anyone. (Know it well)

Keep in mind that study will be enlightened; some of the realtors are so unique that they go with the flow and offer the extra-ordinary care that touches the core of the consumer based on a study of people's behaviour and reaction to the decision made in common life.

Study expands and enlarges the scope of thinking in advanced.

Study the market.

Study the people.

Study results.

This is A system.

Q and A

Q: How often do agents seek help before they run into problems?

A: Not until the problem occurs or has already happened. Why?

Q: Can the problems be solved before they happen?

A: The answer is yes:

Based on the experience, knowing ahead of the problem would lead us to overcome it immediately before it transpired. (A good preparation system is always available)

Note of Failure:

No plan, no goal, no action, no focus, no confidence, no clarity, confusion, don't know what do to, too busy, too many excuses, the list goes on... (Does it have to be like that?)

Rules:

If you don't know where to go, it will take you nowhere.

If you don't go after what you want, you will never have it.

If you don't ask, the answer will always be no.

If you don't step forward, you will always be in the same place.

As we know throughout the history of Real Estate in Canada, Spring and Fall is the most active for buying and selling that involved in many transactions.

If that's the case:

This is the master plan for action that A system must be put in place in which we do not want to miss the timing. (Actions follow by the A system)

Understand the mindset as a top producer / top performer

Understand the business operation and the people's behavior

Understand a realtor's discipline and rules need to be followed.

Understand a realtor's main goals and targets how to work.

Understand what a realtor had to offer and what the client's expecting.

Understand the motivation and focus point of the client.

Understand the total picture or layout graphics with A system plan.

We must put in a massive energy with a serious action in full motion, either we make it or break it during the most crucial time (no excuses).

End of the day, STUDY leads us to knowing what we need to know!

The benefits of working on the listing side of the Real Estate as always!

WHY?

3

LISTING IS THE NAME OF BUSINESS

Over 95% of the sales activities buying or selling came from the report on TRREB were listed on the market as well as major city of Provinces.

All the buyers are working with one form or another through the buyer agent or realtor directly through their purchase.

If you have a listing on the TRREB board or others different boards or within your Brokerage, instantly you have created a serious buyer or through the buyer realtor associate network, which will be generated an agreement of purchase and sale offer through the system provided the circumstance is right.

Imagine if the top listing realtor has a huge database or connections or inventory of the listings, he or she will end up double sales or double deals and, of course, very much possible with triple transactions or more if the landlord or owner decides to look for downsize or upgrade for another property to buy or to lease.... That will reflect the sales activities moving forward that can be generated or produced much more future transactions or deals.

Realtors have a choice to learn to become a great lister and a top producer at their best to improve their skills and manage their time, it's learnable skills and knowledge.

Having a focus point to become a top lister and yet the beauty is they can choose whom they like to work with. (Less stress and more business.)

Every top agent has known and has proven the success of the business fall into a good listing side and build a machine or A system that will lead to a great balance in life for financially, health and mentally framework.

The question is, where to find the right seller or buyer?

Anyone who owns homes is considered a potential seller as well as buyer. (Business is everywhere, especially in the Big City!)

Here are a few ways to find the BUYER for the seller:

If the listing is up on the market for sales with the signage installed, eventually the buyer will be attracted and potentially, a deal can be generated as usual.

Let's look at some ideas:

From the drive-by customer seeing the sign on the lawn,

From the neighborhood area,

From the flyer marketing material,

From the local associate realtor network,

From the online internet media marketing,

From the local newspaper advertising media,

From the info sent to the past client referrals,

From the open house activities done weekly,

Many tools are available out there, use one or more

ideas that are fit our lifestyle to increase our exposure to more business.

Key: To build up a high volume of listing inventory,

A system in place.

Q: Do we have a buyer? Most asked question?

A: Yes... how many buyers do you want?

We know where to find the buyer, this is our day-to-day prospecting on the lists of the buyer through the A system attached here with only a few ways,

Most top lister realtors know how to answer with the right question and ask for the closed.

Q: Who is your buyer? Most Sellers like to know?

A: Buyer came from different area and a great productive listing realtor always works very closely with a handful of buyers or other network buyer's realtor who immediately after the showing or follow up to ask all serious questions and qualify them before an offer is presented.

A system for prospecting schedule is our prospecting tools to follow religiously and almost guarantee or predictable for the realtor with steady income flow and is being part of the work leading into proof of the success.

Proofs:

1. **Theory state of mind** ----everyone has their own set of minds.

2. **Document state of mind**---an official written document is being recorded past, present, and future.

3. **Actual state of mind** ----current actual or current reality or current results

Out of the 3 proofs, the most desired one is for the result the ACTUAL proof or ACTUAL results.

ACKNOWLEDGE by:

Showing the past client testimony with photos and

the contact information is a valid proof of evident or highlighted point.

Showing the royalty staying with the same Brokerage is a focal point along with the success partner with clients.

Showing the clients success in financial improvement in dealing with your service is a plus.

Showing full responsibility and guaranteeing service in writing and under no pressure whatsoever within reason.

Study shown as a buyer/seller likes a person or realtor who is always bright, energetic, charming, optimistic, positive, confident, trustworthy, honest, dignified, sincere and looking good to present and show themselves with all these qualities is a minimum requirement to convince them to use your services and the chances to guide and lead the buyer or seller to the way for the making a wise decision is much higher probabilities.

If it takes what needs to be a good lister, why NOT?

Listing, listing, listing, (skill)

Appointment, appointment, appointment (prospecting).

Presentation, presentation, presentation (showcase).

Follow up, follow up, follow up (reconfirm).

Negotiating, negotiating, negotiating (win-win option).

Closing, closing, closing (asking).

Is it not about who we are? It is about them and is about A system.

How do we do that? Read and study and practice more...

Let's focus on the daily schedule!

4

DAILY SCHEDULE

Every top producer had a very productive layout daily, weekly, and monthly details schedule and, of course, long-term plan as well to be followed. (A system)

The daily schedule function is to show us on the right track without having lost control of our time management or lost sight of the purpose.

A good plan or constructive daily schedule looks like this:

5:00am wake up and get ready for the day.

6:00am light movement, light exercises, practice daily.

7:00am take a hot bath, ready for meditation, prayer, or chanting.

8:00am Full morning breakfast, ready and studying and planning of the activities.

9:00am Block all messages, action in motion, and focus on prospecting clients, finding buyer and seller.

12:00 Break for lunch and 15 minutes walk.

1:30pm Returning same day messages, emails, and phone calls, plus research, or update on MLS market.

3:00pm 30 minutes stretching and light movement and begin to focus on prospecting again.

3:30pm Prospecting on until appointment set.

5:00pm If no appointment set, get ready for the end of the day work, assuming there is an appointment set, try to work around the daytime schedule from 5pm to 8:30pm time range.

Keep in mind, we are ready for next business day.

A new day begins from the repeated daily schedule Mon- Friday.

Every day starts from a new beginning. Start from zero, new business, new focus and new you.

KEY: Success of the day begins with morning schedule hour in action mode.

Hour by hour layout schedule in detail, the more clarity layout, the better position to follow and much easy to reach.

Day by day from Monday to Friday, maintenance work prospecting, prospecting, and prospecting until a qualify listing appointment has been set up.

Prospecting in many forms of the way by phone call, follow up call, past client, past center influence, just listed, just sold, private sales, private rental, or empty nester investor or door knock or flyer distribution or having a scheduled lunch with past clients or meet up with advocate. (Keep talking to the people)

WEEKLY SCHEDULE:

Review the past 5 days' activities, following up with the latest update for clients and the paperwork, open house, viewing homes or showing home with set appointment schedule, getting ready for the following week's schedule.

End of the week, find out what is missing or what is needed to get a better improvement. Was it the people problem, the case issue or the technical things? (Analyze A system)

Knowing from the past, will help to set a greater and brighter stage for the improvement.

MONTHLY SCHEDULE:

Review the goal or target month-end, what needs to be improved, seek for coach advice or one on one discussion with the office Manager or Broker of record and find someone for accountability report or feedback.

A short trip for spring break with the family is part of the plan.

A summertime gets away from 5 to 7 days or 2 weeks vacation is part of the agenda.

A year-end holiday with selected AAA clients is the most ideal plan or

A year-end celebration party with all clients who brought us the business is the right time to be re-connected again and deepen the trust and the relationship for the future business.

Interesting to Know: A Real Life in Real Estate Business

1. New Rookie/New Agent working part or full time:

One or less deal per month must have a coach to start, network from within the office

2. Experienced Realtor/Goal-Oriented:

1 to 4 deals per month must be busy exhausted with buyers, having assistance and a coach is recommended

3. Seasonal Realtor/High Achiever/High Performer:

4 deals above and beyond per month must have A system with a complete layout to build a mini organization.

Q and A

Q: If you don't do this, what would happen?

A: Nothing would happen, nothing will get done,

nothing would achieve, no income generated, going downforce, life is depressed, not happy outcome...

Q: If you do it and don't see the results, what would be next?

A: You must continue to press on, no turning back and keep moving forward, think of the way to work things out. This is the moment to break through, find out what went wrong immediately, look for an answer and find out if is it worth dragging on or get back up and move on.

KEY: Remember every resolution or problems have an answer, we just need to find them, and we know where to locate them. We cannot win all the time, but if we win most of the time, we will reach our goal sooner.

Those are all learnable skills!

Going higher and stronger workload, let's see what needs to be done!

SECTION 2

SOMETHING ACHIEVED THROUGH THE EFFORTS OF A TEAM OF PEOPLE

5

───────

TEAMWORK

Real Estate is a lonely business in a way, when you laugh no one knows, when you are sad no one knows.

You make a huge transaction a big commission is coming on its way, but it doesn't close in the end. (It happened)

You make NO transaction you begin to worry about how to make up the household payment. (It happened)

Youth on fire as always! The spirit of youth is the act or process of moving.

Partnering with the youth will bring enormous result.

Therefore, neither you build A system or within family teamwork or partnering with teamwork with others has proven that with the right desire, focus and motivation, ANYONE can achieve the dream. (BIG TIME)

You become more challenging, especially as a lady realtor working by herself, imagine you have a listing appointment in the Timbuktu area in the evening hour with a stranger? Or you need to do an open house in an outlandish place. (Safety comes first)

However, more so for the future leadership is dominated by the female realtor, you will see a great number of the successful realtor are working with teamwork or A system.

Given the business nature, a single realtor has a limitation on people's power, to work alone and yet want to be a high production performance, it will require 24 hours of work and is easily stressed out.

This is nothing new for create/craft a teamwork plan. It's a future business that many realtors are focusing on and it is also a quicker way that rise to achieve the brand name as you want, plus sending out the messages and showing the youngest energetic plans to empower toward the social media strategy.

End of day, the client deserves the top-notch services and gets to achieve the result, helping the client make the greatest and biggest decision in terms of wealth gains and, in return, the realtor enjoys the true value of the teamwork that delivers excellent service and rewards of satisfaction.

I always enjoy working as a team or partner or hiring my own assistant, the level of energy and focus are always on the right fame of work environment due to the amount of workload that can be demanded or required substantially.

Team commitment creates different thinking, vision and deep in the process of innovative, interesting, and engaging. Many stories and videos displayed records can be used to capture the attention of the public media and is part of the action plan that can incorporate with teamwork.

An investment strategy with A system is a MUST shared plan to make a connection with clients and is part of the plan.

The purpose of the teamwork is to increase sales volume, increase higher income and increase efficiency and increase the benefits for the client.

To find a team player required in A system:

A great team leader or team manager or coordinator is to make sure each team player has the minimum standard to qualify to be part of the teamwork.

e.g.

minimum earning or boost the income is the expectation will be the guideline, willing to learn and be coachable, willing to share and open-minded, more importantly, is to understand the culture and the philosophy of the team leader, the direction of the A system.

For all top producer mindset for having a team or building a team, A system shows the following:

This is the only way was done in the past, now or in the future: to capture the market share due to the populations keep growing and newcomers are increasing.

Three Major Benefits:

1. Team communication and team encouragement.

2. Client communication and client benefits.

3. Lead Generation and business increase.

Let's put into prospective digital workload:

Promotion, advertising, mask media, LinkedIn, Facebook, Instagram, u-tube, WeChat, WhatsApp, individual website, office website, plus many more...

The listing presentation includes a teamwork efforts, for example: installing a lawn sign, inserting a lock box, getting ready to upload MLS listing and making changes periodical, generating flyer material and getting it printed and distributed, get ready for an open houses week day or week end, sending out an invitation or inviting guests for attending the open houses, get ready for the staging set up, more importantly setting up for creating all options available for the multiple bids plus many more handle detailing staffs.

Buying presentation includes a teamwork efforts, for example: require a good driver with a road map direction especially at the busy traffic hours, plus another realtor work closely on showing the property with details information on the facts and figures, an assistant realtor work closely with document preparing for an offer presentation and network with the team partners for banking institute, home inspector, lawyer, mover and many more...all at once narrowing down for the agreement of purchase and sale. (Qualified questions are important before even going out there to view the property)

A perfect team requires each dedicator to live up their spirit, their mission steadfast, true, loyal, devoted, enthusiastic and unity to consider a team of a super star realtor's. (Get the job done)

Team leader or team players are important to look after the needs and concern from the perspective side of the buyer all once at the same time, (Nothing left behind) and the team can do multi-tasks in a different place, at different times and at different clients without delay of any kinds of service.

This is called unity: it is POWER.

Sounds easy in theory, but A system is easy to accomplish!

Keep in mind: do not over promise and under delivery but rather under promise and over delivery is the true value. (We called a good surprise)

Everyone loves GOOD surprises!

Building a team is building an empire is well equal to building a castle of wealth in Real Estate.

Let's look at any size of business operating in this

global world, inside each of these identities always lie A system with TEAMWORK.

Let's look at what do we expect if we were the buyer?

Clients' expectation: A system shows the actual reality and is well organised with the quality work of talented people who show care and pay attention to client's needs and proof of the success of helping others in their portfolio investment by living on the best term and best life. (Do what they say, and say what they do)

Let's look at how to release pressure?

People like to see others show their HAPPY faces!

Key: SMILING is giving the people a warm welcome and is the name of the business as its first perception.

Persistency and patience is endurance for SUCCESS!

Working on determinations is a MUST.

Determinations:

Building a Business with passion and laying a strong foundation is the goal with a strong determination:

My wish is we are determined to help to make a decisive decision.

My wish is we can do it and we believe in it.

My wish is we are willing to do it at all costs.

My wish is we work to achieve the client's target.

My wish is we network with the net worth for the client.

My wish is we know what we want, and we want to share it with the client.

My wish is we work on a clear mindset, emotionally and physically are in top-notch.

My wish is we succeed, the client must come first no matter what.

My wish is we follow the A system faithfully and be transparent to the client.

My wish is we have a vacation getaway trip celebration with the client annually.

My wish is we want to enjoy a steady income and live a high-quality life with the client.

My wish is to determine to put my wish into ACTION.

My action plan for daily work.

My action plan weekly report/review.

My action plan shows actual proof with actual results.

My action plan gets the client involved 100%.

My action plan with 30 days guarantee in written if the client is NOT fully satisfied.

My action plan is fast-acting when concerns or problems arise.

My action plan is to hold the accountability for all my clients.

My action plan is constantly moving forward one case at a time.

My action plan is to propel the client to the next level of the project ONLY if the first is fully satisfied.

My action plan is to get my client's dreams to come true.

My action plan is an execution plan followed by A system.

My action is A system.

To do all these, I must learn to speak like a professional with scripts and dialogue!

6

KNOW THE SCRIPTS

Knowing what to say and how to say, what to ask, when to ask, how to ask are the main communication skills that each salesperson must have and must learn in order to end the closing with a contract signed or purchase order signed.

More we learn to read, remember it, and memorize it. It becomes easy to deliver the right message

Prospective clients know by instinct or by the first impression that when we meet face to face, it shows where you are coming from and what intention you have in mind

As soon as we are clear and clean for transformations, messages are well delivered, so that itself will help to make an easy for acknowledge/acceptance/agree upon by the client .

Each beginning of the conversation will start with and end with the question: does he or she like what we said or the way we propose in the way of our tone, our acts (body language), our look (facial expression), our confidence or comfort level etc.

It's all detected or discovered in our scripts and dialogue!

e.g., assuming he or she is very thirsty and needs a glass of water at that moment, if we offer food instead of water or insist them to eat the food first. You can imagine what kind of response?

This is the beginning of the connectivity, or you might call chemistry in common, that will lead to further toward a good feeling working environment.

As a realtor aware of the question to be asked or been asked is the fundamental knowledge of the practise of the scripts.

Given that the scripts are available and learnable, (Why would we consider looking into them?)

Imagine if we master it like a butterfly, say what you like, ask what you like, lead the client to an understandable and agreeable and acceptable stage, would it be much easier with happy closing. (The power of the scripts is priceless)

For example: some of the scripts are laydown the following pages...

If we are really interested in setting more listings or buying's appointments, see how's the top prospectors overcome objections by knowing and asking the right questions and asking a lot...

Here is the KEY:

To ensure a good contact script.

To ensure a good formula A system they used scripts.

To ensure how the appointment is set even when they get rejected scripts.

All good scripts formats are done by the greatest trainer in the world.

Please look up the site and be ready to join them and

train by the Master and follow the A system and find out who is the right Master for your choice.

KEY: A Top Producer always has a Coach or Master whom they follow for Life.

You will learn the skills, strategies, and tactics of the Top Producer's performance no matter if the market condition is up or down, good or bad, right or wrong.

Most asked question?

Which is more important in terms of performance, the script comes first, or the presentation comes first?

Some said both, what do you think?

Market changes constantly, realtors need to stay abreast at all times.

When to buy?

When to sell?

Should you invest now or later?

How to get my finance ahead?

Let's look at what we need to know on the market.

7

KNOW THE MARKET

Always prepared ahead before the presentation, market includes a CMA, current interest rate and the government interest, personal portfolio, marketing tools, latest update market trends and economic outlook, Brokerage support tools, testimonial from client's update.

Almost everyone seems to know the market or stay on top of the market condition or know someone who is in the real estate business,

Our mission is to keep us on edge to help clients with a true data and insights from the wise market experts, make smart and calculated decisions (When and How?) instead of those based on scary headlines or hearsay, we based on what we had done for the past clients. (Show the proven results)

The KEY: Is finding what is the objective of the client. What is the benefit to offer them?

Knows the market insight equal knowing how to increase wealth for the client!

For example:

If we know there is a mortgage or financial issue with a client, we find a way to resolve it or help to reduce the level of stress with extra options. (isn't what the client is looking for end of the day?)

Knowing the market is knowing the business.

Know when to buy, when to sell.

Know how to buy, how to sell.

Know what to buy, what to sell.

Know who is the most active realtor in the area.

Know who is the most buyer in the area in terms of family income bracket, ages, culture, locally or international.

Know how long it takes to sell or days on market.

Know the rental price in the area.

Know how often the residents move in and out of the area.

Know who are the residents mostly homeowners or investors.

Know the zoning bylaw and land use department in the area.

Know the landscaping and existing roads in the area for future development.

Know what commercial businesses are coming into the area.

Know the demographics and neighbourhood amenities.

Knowing what we know can have an impact change on the decision.

We don't need to know what we know. We need to know what the client needs to know and why?

We cannot take control of the outside world, but we can take control of the decision to be made in a brighter move.

Knowing what and when decisions need to be made is the right move with the knowledge of the realtor

What we need to know are facts and the truth!

Market constantly changes, same as the news and the people think,

Let's work on ourselves internally and faithfully in practise and study, lead us to stay up to the market change for the better and wiser by having A system

Four Essential Steps to Know the Market?

1.Start with Comparative Market Analysis or CMA.

2.A Professional Market Appraisal.

3.Property Market Comparison Tools.

4.Building a Farm area or Market territory and work with local Market realtor.

That's why we have put together the How to Succeed in a changing market and yet stay on the focus of listing side can bring more lucrative revenue in Real Estate business and have a solid client trust-based, especially when times are tough.

Market changes based on many reasons:

A Buyer's Market:

Has more supply than demand, home prices dropped, power of sales increased, foreclosure increased, bank sales increased, new home sales overbuild, this gave buyers more leverage in negotiations

A Seller's Market:

Has created more demand than supply, more buyers become available on the market for a home, less properties for sales creating homes prices skyrocket, this gave sellers more chances in bidding wars and multiple offers on individual properties.

The KEY: Is to find an experienced realtor whose desire is to help the clients create wealth and make the right decision.

End of the day, how we present ourselves shows how successful we are!

8

KNOW THE PRESENTATION

Always being on time for the appointment or staying on schedule is a must, once we rush or are late for the appointment, almost instantly, we lose trust or are not able to do a good job ended up rushing off the presentation.

Everything comes from the 1st connection or 1st approach or 1st handshake or 1st impression to get to know the clients.

Knowing how to present or approach step by step will help the final closing order in a seamless way.

Knowing what to present, what the clients want and what is the motive or motivation is important to find out.

Knowing the presentation consists of price, market value and location.

Knowing the timeline to promote, advertise and sell.

Knowing the reason why, what, and how to achieve together.

Knowing the beginning and the end of the term agreement.

Knowing the next project after sales service.

Knowing the documentation is up to date to be disclosed.

A powerful presentation led the client to follow to the end of making that commitment.

The Story Formula Stated:

I used to be a simple person, no one knows

Until I discovered the right path how to learn and grow

Now I discovered I'm very happy with my system built through my master and I can show you how to do it too.

May I explain it?

Four Most Effectives Way to Play Your Story: (Explain!)

1. Overcoming the difficult thing (Show by Example)
2. Overcoming the fear (Honest and Straightforward)
3. Overcoming the time (Most Valuable is People Business)
4. Overcoming the mindset (Positive Energy)

Three Things to Remember:

1. Know who is your client.
2. Know the beginning and know the end --- what you like to say or how you like to present, our 1st impression is typically involving a positive or negative evaluation.
3. Know what you like to share an ideal's goal or show what you have done for others. (show results)

Presentation required certain criteria:

Do research beforehand, who and what the purpose of the meeting is.

Do research who is the decision-maker.

Do research what are the reason for making that decision.

This will help our communications flow in the direction we want.

This will help to show our professionalism.

Always answer with a Question!

e.g.

The Answer is Yes, may I ask what is the reason?

Presentation is the most powerful tool to get to know the business/client.

Present yourself well.

Present the image good.

Present the knowledge and experience show excellent.

Present the confidence and know-how and why.

Present a clear goal and clear desire.

Everything begins with a strong presentation and ends with strong, easy closing full of positive energy.

KEY: Is to find out by asking the right question and knowing how to ask.

We are there to offer the utmost services acting in between as a middle person to get to the end results for the client and ultimate goal is to have a lifetime relationship for building wealth and living an outstanding happy Life as a good person and bringing the benefit to the client and the society.

Knowing the Client is Knowing Your WEALTH!

9

KNOW THE CLIENT

Always be clear about the purpose of the visit, finding out the needs and wants to provide the services before meeting up.

Know the client well better than they know themselves, with over a 90% of chance they will feel like you are the chosen one.

Clients need to know exactly what you are there to deliver is the solutions or resolve their major concerned.

They want it, you deliver. (Both win)

You offer what they need or get them to accept. (Both agreed)

Business always comes first, show interest to the client.

If the appointment is not qualified, nothing is going to work out

e.g., if you find out the owner is not present, of course, no decision will be made even if we show up at the appointment.

Know them by asking many questions without any bad feelings.

Know why the client needs to buy or sell.

Know what the reason is to buy or sell.

Know when the client like to achieve it.

Know what the client expects.

Know what the options available to make a decision.

Know what the client benefits by working with you.

Know what the client can walk out with the net worth.

Know you can help by helping many others example.

Key: Is to find a solution to resolve the issue or concern and offer hope for a better situation.

Keep in mind most of the reason and issue fall into these categories. (Share with the client, which type are you?)

Moving Up or downside.

Empty nesters sell.

Mortgage issue or overweigh.

Family issue problem.

Health issue concern.

Financial issue difficulty.

Job changes issue or lay-off pressure.

Moving out of town issue or returning home taking care of senior.

Death issue or estate home.

Rental issue no cash flow.

Profit-taking moving to senior home.

Partnership issue split up.

Other's issue did not like to disclose.

If we don't ask, we never know. Let's find out and get to know!

Knowing what specific issue will determine what specific matter to get the job done.

Know the client ---know the business---know the results.

Q and A

Q: What is a Qualified Appointment?

Decision-maker must be present.

They are ready to provide all documents to justify the decision.

They are ready to install lockbox, and signage and be ready for flexible showing appointments.

They have been ready to move since yesterday, have a good reason to move. (Motivated)

Q: What is the Worst Situation?

They decided not to sign the agreement after you had done all your wonderful presentation, qualified all questions and yet they decided to list through someone else.

A: Well, congratulations to them. We move on to the next prospect. (That's why the qualified question earlier on allows us to determine)

KEY: Do not be disappointed or interrupt our emotions, it's part of the business reality, simply just moving forward, however, we can still follow up with them later after the expiry if the home did not sell. What do you think? Why not? Potential future business!

Note of Failure:

Not knowing what to say and how to ask?

Not knowing the latest update on the neighbourhood market conditions.

Not knowing the skills and knowledge, lack the confidence to communicate.

Not knowing the client's wants and needs and who make the decision?

Not knowing well in the business.

Prospective client is seeking the right person to know them WELL. (Why not you?)

To know the client well is to reason with them well.

We have lived in a busy world ever since the high

technology revolution came, constantly bombarded by emails, text messages, and phone calls, news, almost everyone holding their cellular phone 24/7. Information world. This distraction costs us more stress, makes more available info, everyone wants more, lack the quality performance and concentration on what design to be rich in heart.

Our mission is making the client get to know us well benefitting them in returns.

We are just determined to stay more focused on our A system, so we have much to offer.

Today requires ever more for realtors training, let's look at some of them:

SECTION 3

A PLAN OF ACTION DESIGNED TO
ACHIVE A LONG-TERM OR
OVERALL AIM

10

TRAINING

During the past 2.5 years with the pandemics worldwide it was indeed worried and desperate in many ways of our Life and concerned. Who knows how long it will last? It had changed much for our day-to-day business operation. The best time to dive in to learn and train oneself how to cope with the people and business, according to the news, many jobs had been lay-off except working for the front-line public help and essential work, the good news came from Toronto Regional Real Estate market indicated more jobs available in the workforce is building constructions and investing in real estate, therefore more licences have increased and more new Realtors are in the field.

Training is becoming more essential for the service industry.

Many ways of attending the training format, webinars, groups, social events, seminars...

One of the main and most popular during the lockdown period is zoom online video training, it's almost offered different types of daily courses make available for all training in sales, I found this is a great opportunity for oneself to upgrade and boost our thinking into a new way of operations and know-how.

Learning and studying is an ongoing training business, especially in Real Estate.

People business... if we know the people, we know the business. Business is not difficult, only people are difficult.

Training and learning from the office Manager or Broker of Record one-on-one is a way to be coached and understand the culture of people.

Training and learning from the book, will take us far and wide in the depth of understanding the sales activities and performance and the people.

Training and learning from the top producer and offering help from within the office is a goal mind.

Training and learning from a professional speaker, coach or mentor is the most outstanding way toward our goals and accomplishment.

Training and learning sessions is to help us stay on track, support, focus mindset and avoid pitfalls on our journey to success.

Training and learning keep us stay motivated, empowered, connected with other inspiration to achieve the highest potential.

Training and learning and practising in selling are professional jobs in North America and are a highly respected and well paid.

Three Main Keys:

Mentally, Spiritually, and Physically Training is a Basic of all Basics.

Look at those world Olympics performers who work on their daily training schedule easily between 6 to 8 hours per day for months and years just to get to the world stage to compete with others.

(If you want to be the best, do exactly what the best does?)

An intense and serious training on our individual self-discipline must be followed by A system.

Anyone can do it but requires courage, passion, and wisdom.

Given the nature of the business, finding a Master coach is 100% for sure MUST.

Here are Some of the Benefits:

Finding clarity.

Finding accountability.

Building confident.

How to get our desired results faster.

Stay on target.

Best of all, we pay to Learn, We Learn to pay less in the long run.

Given a training opportunity is to expand and grow in our daily life of success.

Training includes self-motivation and being inspired by own individual inspiration are a must to perform a high level of achievement. In other words any sales-person must always stay positive at all given moments of time to help to move the project to the end sales or help the clients to make the right move, having the confidence in us is a fundamental principle.

Required substantial training:

One of the Greatest Trainings in Physical and Mentally form can help Sharpen Our Mind is definitely:

1. Exercises Regularly.
2. Reading Regularly.
3. Practising YOUR faith Regularly.

Training and learning and education is the only way to stay on top of the current market trend, without it, it will properly cost us more loss in terms of earnings in the long run. It does pay for the price of damage or litigations.

People like to stick to the right-minded people to buy or sell or invest, especially with the big items like real estate full of unknown, therefore, positive energy and confidence is part of the training.

An independent contractor or self employ or free-lance who has no system, no custom, no structure, no agenda to follow, no goal setting do simply go with the flow, go with the heart as if whatever it comes, it will take care of itself.

This type of response toward business is not able to expect a high volume production.

We offer FREE live training filled with high energy and enthusiasm to top-performing listing strategies and tactics – unlike anything you've ever seen before from within a group of masterminds that we put together now and, in the future,.

Q and A

Q: How Do You Deal with Negative Attitude Behavior?

A: We try to avoid it as much as possible, or we ignore them completely. (We can't win everyone always and sometimes we must learn and have the courage to say no)

Q: How do you improve negative attitude behavior?

A: Faith, practise, and study.

Having faith in them.

Guide them to the right practise.

Show them study or learn the right materials.

Reference Box:

Note of Failure:

The worst thing is that we never tried, if we don't do it, someone will.

Not well prepared at any given moment.

Not ready for the mindset.

Not taking it seriously enough.

KEY: We should treat our business like a real business, we are the owner, we are self employees, we are a Leader or CEO of a company. Think clearly as if we are head honchos who are responsible for the company to achieve higher and better goals and set the example for the rest.

A system Plan:

1. Have a Plan.
2. Work on a Plan.
3. Focus on a Plan.

Leader Believes in TRAINING!

Let's look at finding the business after the above training!

11

NETWORK WITH AFFILIATED

Are we ready for the common ask questions?

Finding Seller / Owner:

One of the 4 Different Ways:

1. through a referral program.

2. through door knocking.

3. through tech media image.

4. through advocate.

Here are the focus points and here is what we need to understand from the Seller mindset as always looking for and expecting a right answer or perfect answer as follows:

If these were asked, what would be the answer? Are We preparing for these?

Do You Have Any Buyer?

What kinds of marketing plans do you have?

What is your commission charge?

What kinds of advertising do you do?

Someone only charges xxx amount.

Someone only charges a flat fee.

How long does it take you to sell?

How long have you been in this business?

Have you sold any homes here?

I do not see any of your advertising.

I do not want to have a long listing.

I do not want to have an open house.

I do not want to sell or I'm not ready until next year.

I m not the owner of the property?

I m not ready yet until the price reaches xxx amount.

I like to know what my home is worth.

I like to sell and buy, would you cut your commission?

I like to sell and leaseback, can you help?

I like to offer VTB program, can you help?

I like to do a renovation before selling.

I like to put it on the market after my return from my vacation.

I like to speak to my spouse first or my family.

I like to use my previous agent who sold us this property.

I like to interview other agents.

I like to compare with other services.

I like to get free staging, free touch up, free virtual pictures.

I have a relative who is a realtor.

I'm the renter, the owner is related to me, I just passed him the info.

Another part of the owner is out of the country?

The property is owned by the company and I'm not the signing officer.

Plus, many more common ones:

Do you have the right answer now? Can you help and how? Are you capable of handling the job? Can you take the job below the market price, Is the money to be made? Is it worth doing the job? Do you want the job?

Keep in mind all the questions above must have

immediately been satisfied with the right answer to convince the Owner or Seller to get the job done.

Based on a quick reaction using your services dealing with the unknown client or the public.

A system will help to get ready and narrow down right to the point:

Yes, we can or no, we won't!

Q: Where To Find Clients?

A: I have a well runs A system in place, Building teamwork, prospecting daily according to the daily, weekly, and monthly schedule.

Keep talking to people.

Anyone can be a potential seller only if the motivation is in place. E.g. (A system plan and action plan)

Through my proactive act on Expiry listing, Private sales, open houses, neighbourhood active sales activities for past months, referrals, database, website, mask media, online links many ways and many sources.

Through office group site or network, WeChat, WhatsApp.

Through associate Realtor's network.

Through flyers advertising.

Through my custom make the video display.

Through my pre-listing package.

Q: Does it Matter To Work with An Experienced Realtor?

A: The answer is YES, absolutely (Do You Know The Difference)?

End of the day, what would be the expectation from the Seller's?

Finding Buyer/Purchaser:

One of the 4 Different Ways:

1. through people network.

2. through social media.

3. through a strong marketing program.

4. through listing online system.

Certain steps must take to qualify the buyer:

Here are the focus points and here is what we need to understand from the Buyer as they are always looking for their own interest.

Let's build A system for a heart to hearts dialogue for the questions most asked as follows:

Instead of having the answer to any questions, we rather suggest to the buyer and ask for half an hour to an hour meet up or an interview appointment by both the buyer and the agent.

(Note: very important to qualified for a buyer's)

This reason for the meeting is that the buyer and the agent are both satisfied with each other, understand the services representing the client verse customer, and each liability that is involved benefits the client by working with the realtor.

Building a rapport, understanding the relationship and exchange of ideas.

This will allow both sides to decide whether it is worth the time to spend together for searching a home for the prospective buyer by having a clear vision and a clear understanding of where the value to be created or even for the benefit of the buyer to agree and willing to pursue to the next level or even further.

As it turns out does it mean to be working together in the first place?

This is an outstanding professional approach for each meeting working with Buyer/Purchaser. Within 10 to 60 minutes, both ends will find out exactly what is the process or purpose of the meeting.

(It works well with the top producer with A system)

The groundwork layout is fundamental in creating a

human-to-human connection with a deep bond of under-standing what might be transpired during the transaction take place.

The clearer of the picture, the better flow of the process and created good chemistry that led to the closing of the commitment.

Q and A?

As a realtor or agent for clarification questions and motivation is a qualified question.

Here are some of the direct and most common asked question as follow:

Are you currently working with any other agent?

Are you renting now or owning a home?

Is the fund ready for closing or ready for deposit?

Are you available for the closing?

Are you buying new or resale?

Are you buying a condo or townhome or semi or detached?

How long have you been looking to buy?

What is your budget and comfort level?

What exact home are you looking to buy? Why?

What size of the home prefer? Why?

What area are you prefer? Why?

What time and date do you prefer to view the home?

Why are you buying?

How soon do you like to own a home? Why?

Who are you working with for your mortgage finance?

Who will be on the title of the property?

Who will be signing the contract or agreement of purchase and sale?

Who will be helping to make the decision?

Who do you use for the lawyer?

There is a reason why the above question is so important for us to get to know each other, helping you to find the right property, the more criteria you want and needs, the better search I can dive into finding, by having these short meeting will save a lot more time for the big investment.

Sometimes what we want and need do not go well together.

e.g., you might want a double garage, but you don't need it for now and therefore can have a impact on the prices or the budget.

This applies party to ask all questions related!

Let us find out what we should know about what transpired in real estate buying and selling a home?

We will find out our discussion plan as follow:

e.g.

Time can be an issue, Sellers like to sell and close in 6 months' time, but you can't wait, and you loved the house, and you want it now or 2 months from now. What's next?

As a buyer is most interested in knowing, what is in for ME:

Buyer's realtor preparing with a good plan program will help you eliminate a lot of hassle or inconvenience. No surprises later or any misrepresentative; however, it should be full of joy and happiness in carrying out the process right to the end search.

Let's find the reason why!

Most buyers wish to purchase their home through someone they know as related to many years of friend-ship relationship or through referrals; however, some-times it will end up quite a challenging situation due to money privacy involved. It could be an uncomfortable situation, sometimes totally lost or disconnected with one another or even lost the relationship period because of non-disclosure, unfortunately I have seen it in my years of practise, quite often is due to monetary and over-looked details privacy involved.

Let me explain what you need to know as a representative on your behalf: (Note: it is very important for the buyer to know that more transparency is, more disclosure is better understanding of feeling created and building trust in relationship.)

Preparing the agreement of purchase and sale for an offer, what form is required to sign and accomplished. Explained?

Preparing the sum of the certified deposit fund within 24 hours upon acceptance of an offer.

Preparing multiplex offer presentation situation, how?

Preparing a firmed no condition offer, are you ready?

Preparing a financing and home inspection clauses, explained?

Preparing a lawyer's final approval review, recommended?

Preparing a status certificate review by the lawyer, why?

Preparing a final visit prior to the closing, why?

Preparing a fund transfer and final document signing, are you ready?

Preparing a final closing pick-up key, time, and location. I will be there, why?

Preparing a mover and changing of address update, is a must prepared ahead.

A true buyer agent walks you through from the beginning all the way to the final step of pick-up key owning a home. Preparing a housewarming party soon or celebration will be arranged.

This is so important to explain to the buyer know what kind of services we will deliver and what form of incentive or commission or pay we are getting throughout this time and is a moment to highlight rebate, reward, and referral fees.

Remember our realtor to do not get paid until the final closing takes place or commission is paid. If anything happens in between courses the transaction is not able to close, we will go back to the square one. What that means is we realtors are taking it seriously to perform doing the job as professionals to follow the rules and regulations under the guideline of RECO or different jurisdictions.

Although the commission came from the seller's side, the buyer does not pay for it, but we realtors are expecting in returns of the buyer's full commitment, therefore the reason for meeting up face to face getting to know all the terms in the agreement of purchase and sales what need to change, or update will openly layout on the table for discussion as suppose we should be moving forward or not.

There isn't any obligation or cost for the first meet up unless the right decision makes to move forward working together, one of the foremost requirements is buyer agency agreement (BRA) need to be established and explained to avoid complication later.

As a realtors, our job is not to sell any tangible item, we are simply providing the services and knowledge, acting as a middle person to put a deal together based on the buyer and seller are willing to accept or reject the property sales.

Putting us in a better position than we are in together for making that purchase for the biggest investment of the home, make no mistake, we will be more satisfied with the buying process.

Knowing what the next step is ahead will always put

us in a better negotiating stage to benefit to the buyer's side.

For example:

Finding out what is the motivation of the seller.

Knowing when the right timing is to send in the offer.

Knowing how the best communicates with the listing realtor or what needs to ask and discuss.

Last but not least, to keep in mind as such:

Buyers need to set aside of the fund for the closing fee.

e.g., lawyer fee, land transfer tax, disbursement fee, property tax (if applicable), moving cost, mortgage expanse or cost (if 2nd or 3rd lender) Etc.

A system will help to increase the buying process!

Q: After The Transaction is Done, What's Next?

A: Finding a second or sound investment or an opportunity for ready to execute or ready for building a strong portfolio is the right time yet to plan.

End of the day, what would be the expectation from the Buyer?

Four Ways System To Increase Wealth:

1. Understand good clients/good people.

2. Understand what people want.

3. Understand where to find it for them.

4. Understand how to get it or execute it.

Most questions that the buyers like to know:

What is it for them?

What if I find the property on my own?

What happens if I brought a new property without a notified realtor?

What is my obligation not to work with a realtor after signing the BRA?

What if I brought it directly with the listing brokerage?

What if I brought it through the open house?

What if I change my mind after signing BRA?

What if not able to get my finance to approve?

What if I'm not getting my price?

What if my family does not agree?

What if I like to back out of the deal?

What if I change my mind and do not proceed with the deal?

What if my fund is not arriving on time for closing?

What if the inspector finds some deficiency?

Note: it is very important to cover all the concerns of the buyer's legitimate questions by developing an understanding through communication and building a strong rapport.

(What if) questions should be discussed in detail face to face meet up agenda. This way, we could move ahead without any misunderstanding in a better and comfort manner, or decisions can be made easier with a yes deal or no deal.

Does it make sense for that meet up? I think so!

As professional realtors, we prefer to have this meeting set up!

This s a great way to show as a professional realtor how we take good care of details for each client under the scope of investment, not only for one transaction, hopefully more with multiple units on return of income (R.O.I).

To maximize the R.O.I and reduce the risk.

A system is where the experienced team depending on.

The KEY here is Win-Win Results.

After all, is part of the RECO requirement for fully disclosed and fully acknowledged before any signing.

Think of professional jobs like a doctor, lawyer, accountant, engineer, pilot, teacher, architect, and others.

These professional people always ask questions foremost before they decide to take the job or decline. Never have I seen any of these professionals begin to take the job without knowing what the client wants.

KEY: The buyer has the right to accept or refuse to work with the realtor.

Then, now, coming to the Future Outlook:

Q: How to succeed in a changing REAL ESTATE market with ongoing uncertainty and noise?

The Time:

Timing is everything and very important in Life. Let's look at the lifespan in general:

The day we're born until 20 years: graduated from high school.

20 to 30 years: graduated from university. (some might drop out earlier)

30 to 40 years: creating a family and building a career at the same time.

40 to 50 years: success and failure were determined as a result.

50 to 60 years: reward with success or continue with the challenge.

60 to 70 years: success with a joyful career and planning for an easy life of retirement or continuing with limited challenge and with limited courage.

70 to 80 years: Time to reflect on the journey of lifespan. (Often, we heard or said if I could have another 20 years time, it will make a difference? Sound familiar?)

80 to 100 years: the next 20 years is the most crucial time. HEALTH is what life aspires for and family love and comfort are what we all want in life. This will tell

what we are living with a full of success stories or they aren't anything to talk about.

The time that has passed can never be regained. Great achievements can only be realized by continuously seizing opportunities when they present themselves and giving one's full force or full attention to doing what must be done.

Misuse of time or not being able to manage our time correctly is almost making our life not moving forward and will take us to detour in our journey of success, regrettable later in life.

Creating a well-planned, well-organised, well in advance will take us to full of abundance. (Find out or speak to the senior experienced)

Time is the most essential asset and will not wait, stop, relax and so on... Moving second by second regardless of where we are and who we are, it's just time passing by instantly and moving forward endlessly without hesitation.

If you do not value it, it will be gone with the wind and no return forever. (It is sad but is reality)

THEY SAID: Success comes with the right time, the right moment, and the right place.

Almost everyone is living short of time, not enough time to accomplish what we want.

Many of us are living and dealing with multiple tasks, how to manage them and get things done is constantly a challenge and is become part of our busy daily life.

Since we have it, we must well use it, we must well spend it, we must well control it with A system plan.

The universe has its own system.

The country has its own system.

The family has its own system.

The individual has its own system.

The core is A system, work on A system, analyze it, expand it, modify it, understand it, A system will take shape and natural form into A automation platform.

When A system is put into an action plan, everything will start to move in direct motions.

KEY: do not hold on to the past, we cannot change the past, we can learn from the past and become better.

The important thing is to create a better future.

Do you think you need to have A system plan?

THEY SAID: a new version of SUCCESS comes with no time, at anywhere and at anytime.

Change the INNER SELF, everything runs the way You want it to Run.

Study TIME is value

The people:

People are the most important assets; everything is started or created by the people and contributes back to the society.

They said: success comes with connecting with the right people, the right product, and the right value.

Everyone wants something today in a rush manner, or they have wanted it since yesterday without patients or much waiting.

A professional realtor always gets exactly what the client wants in a short amount of time and seamless way to the result

In order to win in life for the people's hearts, people's souls, people's emotions, we can transform all the processes into tangible assets.

Today's world we live in is an ever busier life, much so to treasure the value of people. You just don't know who can bring you that advantage, good or bad. People buy or sell through emotion feeling however as a great realtor, we are moving ahead one step forward if we have A system plan.

A great system plan is a must with boundless benefit win-win for all.

Success People Enjoy Balancing Life in 3 Things:

1. Success in Work Life.

2. Success in Family Life.

3. Success in Self Awaken Life.

If we can achieve the 3 things above in Life, you have enough financial resources to pay for your living expenses and allow you to afford many of your Life goals without having to work or otherwise commit any of your time or efforts to generating MONEY.

In Today's world, people wanted to learn from the best and be surrounded by successful people, trying every means to work hard, work sharp to get to the top, ultimately, all people themselves are capable individuals and potentially have room to grow as a truly human being, successful in life.

As what they said: to make a huge impact in people's life .

Is it not what you know, how much you know?

Is WHO you know, WHO you can trust,

Meeting the right people, right teacher, right mentor, right coach, right partner, right trusted counselor, right experienced senior person can change our career in Life. Especially a Master in Life. (How to find one?) by asking, searching, finding...

The right mentoring relationship can be a powerful tool for professional growth ---it can lead to a new job, a new promotion, new leadership to greater success, or even a better Work-Life Balance.

KEY: to put all the 100% of the energy and stay

focused like a laser on a current mission or doing a job to be accomplished one step at a time with full attention.

Study PEOPLE is an asset.

The Speed:

Everyone wants a thing done now or immediately.

A way of acceptance or to make a quick decision is to provide an easy understand and feeling comfortable is the ONLY way to accept and agree and is the fastest the solutions to commit.

The goal is to give you the service you need, when you need it, we want to provide that service in a custom make.

e.g.

Dedicated driver services for showing activities.

Dedicated modern technology /online service communications.

Dedicated manpower leadership services

Dedicated same-day excellent service within a designated area.

Dedicated in-person integration services.

Dedicated time is the decisions making.

Dedicated a fast action to get thing done.

Three Points to Memorize:

1. To listen is to close more sales.

2.To write is to remember.

3.To act is to experience.

Study SPEED is an action.

Working with Partnership Affiliated or associated as follows:

1. Lawyer is an important partnership: (How)

Ideally is to increase the relationship to help and resolve any problems that arise in exchange for building the trust for a future strong business network for investment.

Interrelationship of exchange business as always meaning ideas plan for business partner opportunity.

Ideal for sharing seminar program.

Ideal for client privilege benefits.

Ideal for commercial and residential Real Estate.

Ideal for seeking legal advice or counsel on a legal matter.

Ideal for what is legal right to deal with people in general.

Ideal for easy to find a partner.

Ideal for extra income revenue.

2. Home Mortgage Brokers are the backbone of the transaction. (How)

He or she is playing an important role here to get right down to the financial core, not only for the buying a new or resale home or selling the current home or porting from one mortgage to another, more importantly, are getting the deal approved in a timely matter.

Capable for the future expansion on investment and building a strong credit foundation as well.

The more leverage to the end-user, the brighter the future for the client.

A well experienced and dedicated person will help to generate a wonderful future for the client in exchange for offering a great return business in addition to offering more to the realtor for the power of sales or bank sales or distress sales with many other products to increase the revenues net worth

A network of fundraising.

A network of building wealth.

A network to maximize the leverage.

A network of increase of profit-making.

A network of reconciliation of debts

A network of building wealth is the KEY

3. Home inspector:

Honestly is the best policy to give an effective communication report, detailing report is not always a good report rather than the easy understanding term based on the main key points illustrate what can and how to resolve or replace or options with the least damage.

Comprehensive package.

Drone service:

A fully inspected home before the sale is a great plus

A fully licensed/certified.

A fully responsible and full report immediately.

A full honor guarantee.

A fully experienced contractor.

He/she can be a saver or killer, is who you choose.

He/she can be an excellent advocator.

He/she can be a problem solver.

He/she can be a money maker.

4. Home renovations:

A handyman person with good knowledge and an experienced and good reputation can help to build wealth for ALL (including salesperson, clients, and handymen) together

By working hand in hand, it can be developed into a business partnership adventure.

e.g.

A great handyman turns into a small developer alongside with investor client and with the help or presented by the right salesperson for developing strategies in working together.

Handyman in use.

Demolish and replacement.

Knowledge of permits and inspections requirement.

Home remodelling services.

Complete project from start to be finished.

A free quote in writing.

A qualified proof and licence.

An actual proof of work.

A great partner to be with for building lucrative revenue.

5. Home mover:

This is a great connection with locally and international company who always looking for services of buying and selling real estate through salesperson and they do offer daily rental, weekly or long-term services on all types of vehicles

They provide number of people mover.

They provide warranty insurance and certified program.

They provide packaging box and supplies.

They provide storages short or long term.

They provide any sizes of vehicles to accommodate.

They provide a good advocator / free estimation.

They provide full service, stress free moving program.

They provide hourly service.

They provide referrals program or incentive.

6.Central of influence:

We called those people who can boost our market access and credibility through referrals, testimonials, and word-of-mouth. In other word, these are representatives who can go out an extra mile to your network, their network and go beyond to either way say good thing about your service. A friend for Life!

Being a realtor, a good system takes you far and beyond the scope of imagination or the concepts of external fortune.

How we can utilize them to maximize the profit sharing.

People in charge of church/church leader.

People of the head of community/local businesses.

People of the organisation/group.

People of friends and family members.

People of past client and current client.

People of passion and care and felt trust, honest and positive experience from your service.

People of genuine interest.

People of networking wealth.

7.Working with builder / developer---how to increase realtor revenue? Open suggestions.

Get an exclusive right to promote and market the product.

Get a fully exposure to the marketing plan.

Get your manager and brokerages involved.

Get a solid and secure contract or work sheet on each submission.

Working with different realtor outside the box.

Working with locally, national, and international connections.

Have a strategic plan of advertising exclusively.

Have a great invitation seminar along with Builders.

Have a great and powerful team looking at all level of services.

More importantly get the builder to initial or suggest having a complete fully furnish with ready move in condition. It will help new buyer or newcomer to make a quicker decision based on what they see, what they get (custom make). One price-one move-one sale. Like a model suit.

Builders prefer as always as quick, fast, clean, and efficient firmed deal.

Great way to increase revenue for client and investor as well.

8.Working with farmland, vacant landowner (How)

Searching on land legislation on local municipalities, visit the office.

Finding out through neighborhood / local community.

Finding out network connection.

Finding out through a board program source.

Finding out the owner motivation to sell.

Finding out what benefits to sell.

Finding out what there to offer.

Finding out the urgency for the land scarp changes.

Finding out the supply and demand update.

Finding out who will be interested to buy.

Finding out through mortgage broker source.

Finding out the lease back program.

Finding out the right to own 1st priority after sale.

9. Working with commercial, office, industry owner lease and sale. (How)

Searching for the owner contacts through local registration department, visit the site.

An expiry MLS listing.

A promotion marketing tools.

An immediate buyer is interested and are ready for an offer present.

A realtor yourself is a buyer or lease.

An investor or group is ready buyer or lease.

A buyer or lessor agency is in place.

A data based on the portfolio.

A words of mouth referral.

A lease tenant is a buyer now or vice verse.

A starter new business owner or newcomer.

A management office.

An exclusive network with local realtor.

10. Working with rental management building. (How)

A great referral program in place.

A great supervisor or superintendent from within the building.

A great office data based for clients.

A great department for specialize rental leases.

A well experienced realtor or specialty.

A well exposure signage.

A proven results and fully documented contract.

A well credit tools for credit report.

A well manage of the side trade.

A well promotion advertising program for tenant.

A well knowledge of permit restriction guideline.

A proven result on rentals.

A great incentive programs.

A great team in place.

11.Working with architecture designer, how to create for an extra income or more business occur. (How)

An exclusive referral programs.

An exclusive agreement offers.

A well-known renowned client.

A proven record testimonial with small, medium, and large projects.

A great idea for incentive program.

A great connection investor qualified buyer.

A great connection with financial institution.

A great network oversea buyer.

Note of Success and Failure:

Proactive and creative create abundance with courage and wisdom.

Being reactive are simply waiting for things to unfold before responding. (Unprepared)

Summary

A layout details plan is a must for A system in place to run as auto pilot.

A strong energy is a must stay positive.

A strong and sharp focus point is a must.

Future Business is a must on teamwork, team efforts, partnership, master mind group to be formed to create unity for business expansion.

Leveraging each team member is a must to cultivate individually talent to be formed as team spirit.

Leveraging the technology tools is a must to advance for promotion and networking exposure.

Honest policy system is a must to build trust among people. Understand people is understand Business, getting what the client wants is win-win situation on the right path to succeed.

People buy or sell through feeling, emotional reaction decision, if we care enough to find out the right solution to the concerned, the chances are, we will end up with more contract signed or more sales.

Success come with dedication and discipline along with A System.

Always follow up by asking past client to help us to build our future business.

Always staying in touch with working with referrals business.

Always build our testimonial profile along with success story.

Always looking to think of profit sharing with good people.

Always looking to help others to achieve their goal first.

Always there to provide care before others.

Always stay flexibility and adaptability but to show the value.

Always willing and able to commit for the client.

Always respond quick when there is an issue.

A brief introduction on myself

I wish I have a mentor or coach in my early stage of real estate career, it takes a long journey to learn the hard work and persistence, having A system, having skills and knowledge is the only way to go. Learning and education speed up the process but you paid to learn if not there will be cost more down the road and is it worth it? The answer is as always: YES

In the early 80' work as busboy, waiter, assistant chef and became a chef, it did not work out well, came into salesforce, selling automobiles, selling roger's cable, selling clothing business, selling advertising signage, and developed as a business owner operation for manufacturing signage, retail, and sales service in a small skill industry.

In early 90' I joined in real estate market in Toronto hoping to do well in this career, went out and studied and got my sales license. I always thought if it did not work out well, I have a 2nd plan in my portfolio is selling aeroplanes!

Indeed, it lasted till now in the 21st century. I recalled within the first month, I wrote up 5 listings contract with the unknown clients, I knew this is it, I like it, I love it and I enjoy it. Ever since then, I have stayed focused on my listing side of the business.

As they said: you list and you last, listing is the name of the business. No listing = No sale. You don't last long; you will be an employee as you are supposed to be an employer!

In the early stage of the real estate business, you see

the most couples are husband and wife who work hand in hand, helping one another is common, I studied the trend and the movement of the activities and took a further step to begin the teamwork action plan and believed that I'm the first who have initiated the first-ever build teamwork system in the mid 90', it ended way over my expectation in term of the much better services delivery and higher performances were achieved and get more done and much to offered with much higher income resulted.

Soon after, I became a top lister for Re-max.

Soon after, we became the top team for Homelife.

Soon after, I became the president of my own Home-life Brokerage.

Soon after, I buy and sell within my personal portfolio over 16 properties in less than 10 years period.

Soon after I had gone sidetracked into a stock market, my vision gave me a delusion and confusion. Indeed, it turns up not a healthy environment.

Since I returned to the sales force and started working at the management level by doing training, coaching, recruiting, and learning as time and the business evolved, I have been sharing all my experiences, skills, and knowledge to help build on my ideas in this career by strongly working together as a teamwork to stay focus on one path only. (listing)

I'm fortunate and, as always, love to share and exchange the right mindset for building A system in these constantly changing worlds. Being a CEO of one of the Homelife Brokerage, within a year time in 2021, we were awarded one of the top listed Brokerage in whole of Canada.

A system involves great people and a great mind and great heart, each individual talent and wisdom that are put together into the right system created a powerful and distinguished result.

Along these many years of my career in the Real Estate Business, I strongly believe the pie is too big to accomplish on your own if we want to do well. In my opinion, every salesperson will get a fair share only if we build A system or have A system!

A lifelong career depends on the right system.

Peaceful way to support each other from internal within the office is a beginning way as well as from external with other Brokerages by getting the deal done successfully and happily for the Buyer and Seller is the utmost important task equally to get a listing agreement signed.

I do not find any reason to create complications on the issue or fight against each other simply of our eagle in place. After all, we realtors are governed by the Real Estate Council of Ontario (RECO) or within their own jurisdictions by law.

Having fun selling and enjoying reading this book and applying the principles will refine your approach and work on your goal that will make the difference in the life of consumers and the growth of the business or career.

Ultimately FAITH is the most important in any endeavor in Life, no matter what is your believed.

I'm happy and honored to be appreciated with much of the support came from the comrade, associate or friend who is given me a lot of input and ideas to put together this book and thanks to my publisher, my editor and of course, my Wife and daughter (Elaine and Leslie) and my family Brothers and Sisters.

I'm a Buddhist in the faith of Soka Gakkai International (SGI) organisation with over 192 countries and territories worldwide, practicing, and chanting Nam Myo Ho Renge kyo for the sake of humanity based on Peace, Culture, and Education. Thanks to the Leaders and Members for their many years of encouragement in my practise of faith.

My Mum had been unable to receive much education as a child, and as such, had difficulty writing, however, she began to study in earnest by putting into practice what she learned, she eventually was able to improve her handwriting so much that it was even praised by others.

Quotes from Daisaku Ikeda's published works:

This lifetime will never come again, it is precious and irreplaceable. To live without regret, we must have a concrete purpose, continually setting goals and challenges for ourselves. And we need to keep moving toward those specific targets steadily and tenaciously, one step at a time. (www.sokaglobal.org)

With Respect:

Any Comment or Feedback or Suggestion or Expansion or Exchanging ideas direct to the email at ychoy3@gmail.com

The future is waiting for you NOW.

The future is ever BRIGHT.

The future is dependent on YESTERDAY.

The future is full of OPPORTUNITIES.

The future is HERE.

The future is YOU.

The Future Belongs to Those Who Have The Courage and Wisdom.

. . .

The truth of the matter:

Finding oneself or seeing oneself through oneself is an education process.

Until we know who we are, understand oneself and know oneself deep and well, it will become easy to get to the highest self perfections and be attracted to the goodness of things in Life but it requires A system. (Let's build it)

Building a great business or working toward our goals in Life is building oneself daily, weekly, and monthly or yearly moment by moment, building the momentum in the core!

KEY: Carrying a Blueprint with A System Plan, the Foundation of the Base is the Future Solidity Vision.

A System is ahead of the game!

Freedom of Time is TRUE LIVING!

Have a Great Wonderful and Joyful Journey in Real Estate.

My personal website: www.ontario-lands.com

GREAT SERVICE WITH GREAT COMMENTS

'Well written until I saw the plan, I'm in the master Mind group, we talk about Passive Residual Income. This is THE big opportunity for anyone who wants to create a retirement plan.'

Jonathan Ly, President, and CEO of CARSON ASIA GROUP LIMITED

'To help many agents replace their transaction income with REFERRAL FEE income and retire in the next few years. Awesome!'

Mohammad Piroozfard, Broker of Record Homelife Golconda Max Investment Realty Inc.

'Simple success strategy, unity is strong and creates multiple resources to help to sell more homes, lower your liability and increase your retention.'

Ned Allam, President, Array International Architects, Toronto

'Education, Training and Technology is the way for the future to teach and share these methods. I Have to admit, this is impressive to me. A lot of agents are bringing home more money right off the bat.'

Karen Cai, President of Homelife Golconda Realty Inc.

Sponsor by: Homelife Golconda Realty Inc.

HOMELIFE GOLCONDA
Realty Inc., Brokerage*
* Independently Owned and Operated
HIGHER STANDARDS
Bus: 905-888-8819 Fax: 905-727-9899 Web: www.homelifegolconda.com

www.ingramcontent.com/pod-product-compliance
Lightning Source LLC
Chambersburg PA
CBHW020744160726
47993CB00006B/2600